When I Was A GIRL... I Dreamed

Written by

Margaret Baker & Justin Matott

Illustrated by

Mark Ludy

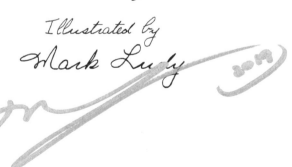

Scribble & Sons
GoodBookCo.com

When I was a girl, I dreamed great dreams

of who I'd be and where,

of places near and journeys far,

adventures wild and rare.

I dreamed I was the teacher,

of an eager, lively class.

I taught them reading, writing, math,

and prayed they all would pass.

*M*any of my students

led extraordinary lives.

Imagine my joy when one naughty boy

received the Nobel Prize!

I dreamed I was a dancer,

so graceful, so refined.

Directors longed to sign me on,

and roles for me designed.

I jumped and twirled up on my toes.

I leapt and soared so high.

A princess in my pale pink shoes,

I felt like I could fly.

I dreamed I was an artist,

studied brushstrokes, mastered hues,

and painted on my canvas

the world's most splendid views.

My landscapes were in great demand.

The art world knew my name.

What a delight to know my work

had earned such lasting fame.

I dreamed I cared for animals,

for every kind of beast,

from the strong and mighty rhino

to the smallest and the least.

*M*y patients came from far and wide,

from every stripe and nation.

I even cured the jungle king!

(I had quite a reputation).

I dreamed I built a robot

who could vacuum, cook and clean.

She even washed my windows!

What a marvelous machine.

*S*he'd paint my nails and comb my hair,

then fix my supper, fast.

A fantastic friend, my robot maid,

we really had a blast!

I dreamed I was a diver

who explored the seas down deep.

I studied coral reefs and sea life

and exotic things that creep.

S uch an awesome mass of fish,

each one with its own style.

What a joy to take close-ups

and to see that great white smile.

I dreamed I floated 'round the world

in a huge hot air balloon.

From L.A. to New York

on a sunny afternoon.

I saw mountains, valleys, cities, towns,

and oceans shore to shore.

All Seven Wonders of the World,

then discovered several more.

I dreamed I lived in Egypt,

seeking artifacts so rare.

I burrowed under pyramids

to see what might be there.

*A*nd what I found, you won't believe,

deep beneath the earth,

The Tomb of the Five Kings!

Of immense and untold worth.

I dreamed I had a clubhouse

that was stationed up in space.

I invited all my friends to come

to that exciting place.

*W*e'd play volleyball and checkers,

talk at poolside, share a snack.

Though it was far, my rocket car

would zoom us there and back.

I dreamed I rode my faithful horse

out in the wild Wild West.

I rounded up the bandits,

and proved I was the best!

I hauled those villains into town

and restored the rule of law.

Was presented with the city's key.

The mayor was in awe.

I dreamed I was an athlete,

playing basketball for "State."

That season we won every game.

Our teamwork was first-rate.

*W*e made it to the finals,

all tied, the clock near zero.

I jumped, I aimed, I shot,

I SCORED! That night I was the hero.

I dreamed I owned a shopping mall,

and went on quite a spree.

I bought odds and ends for all my friends,

and even some for me.

S hoes and purses, jewelry, hats,

in boxes stacked so tall.

With a pair of dapper butlers

at our every beck and call.

I dreamed I was the President,

the leader of my land.

My goal was not to rule,

but rather seek to understand.

*A*nd so I listened closely,

read each postcard, every letter.

And together with all citizens,

we made our country better.

I dreamed that I wrote stories

of princesses and lords.

I even won a Newbery

and other book awards.

*B*ut the notes my readers sent to me

gave me far more pleasure.

To know that I'd inspired their hearts,

that is my greatest treasure.

$\mathcal{Y}$es, as a girl I dreamed great dreams.

Perhaps you dream them too.

Reach higher than the stars, my dears,

and your dreams...

will come true.

For Lauren, who I love and believe in . . .
completely. - ML

For my lovely niece Cee Cee, If I dreamed I had a daughter,
that dream would be you! - JM

For Adela, Elaina, Faith and Zannah Rose. - MB

Illustrator

MARK LUDY is the writer and illustrator of several books. With a style all his own he creatively reaches audiences everywhere, be it through his books, his art or his speaking. With a hilarious sense of humor he engages people of all ages. Mark is happily married with three children. Discover more about him and his new works at **MARKLUDY**.COM

Author

JUSTIN MATOTT is the writer of many books including "When I Was A Boy . . . I Dreamed." He is a passionate soul who loves what he does and it shows. He is a regular speaker in schools and has the ability to communicate with kids in such a way that they "get it." Justin lives in Highlands Ranch, Colorado. Be sure to discover all Justin's book at **JUSTINMATOTT**.COM

Author

MARGARET BAKER is the mother of five and is married to the "man of her dreams." She loves kids, ice skating and reading stories to children. She is a Princeton/Harvard graduate with a Ph.D in Chinese Literature. This is her first book. She lives in Ann Arbor, Michigan.

2013 Paperback Edition

Scribble & Sons
www.GoodBookCo.com

Scribble & Sons is an imprint of Green Pastures Publishing , Inc.

Baker, Margaret.
Ludy, Mark.
Matott, Justin.
When I Was A Girl... I Dreamed/Justin Matott; illustrations by Mark Ludy
Summary: An older woman tells of the extraordinary dreams he had as a young girl.
But were they dreams at all, or perchance tales from an amazing life still being lived?

ISBN-13: 978-0615932866
ISBN-10:061593286X

Printed in USA

Other wonderful books by author/illustrator Mark Ludy

CPSIA information can be obtained
at www.ICGtesting.com
Printed in the USA
LVHW071332110219
607131LV00012B/314/P

* 9 7 8 0 6 1 5 9 3 2 8 6 6 *